GREAT AMERICAN

HORSES

AN IMAGINATION LIBRARY SERIES

PALOMINOS

To Clinton Township Library:

Janet Perry

by Victor Gentle and Janet Perry

Gareth Stevens Publishing
MILWAUKEE

For a free color catalog describing Gareth Stevens' list of high-quality books and multimedia programs, call 1-800-542-2595 (USA) or 1-800-461-9120 (Canada). Gareth Stevens Publishing's Fax: (414) 225-0377. See our catalog, too, on the World Wide Web: gsinc.com

Library of Congress Cataloging-in-Publication Data

Gentle, Victor.
  Palominos / by Victor Gentle and Janet Perry.
    p. cm. — (Great American horses: an imagination library series)
  Includes bibliographical references (p. 23) and index.
  Summary: Describes the physical characteristics and appearance that a palomino horse has, how these horses are bred, and some famous palominos.
  ISBN 0-8368-2133-5 (lib. bdg.)
  1. Palomino horse—Juvenile literature. [1. Palomino horse. 2. Horses.]
I. Perry, Janet, 1960- . II. Title. III. Series: Gentle, Victor. Great American horses.
SF293.P3G45   1998
636.1'3—dc21   98-14793

First published in 1998 by
Gareth Stevens Publishing
1555 North RiverCenter Drive, Suite 201
Milwaukee, WI 53212 USA

Text: Victor Gentle and Janet Perry
Page layout: Victor Gentle, Janet Perry, and Renee M. Bach
Cover design: Renee M. Bach
Series editor: Patricia Lantier-Sampon
Editorial assistants: Mary Dykstra and Diane Laska

Photo credits: Cover, pp. 5, 9, 11, 13, 15, 21, 22: © Bob Langrish; p. 7: © Barbara von Hoffmann/Tom Stack and Associates; pp. 17, 19 © The Kobal Collection.

Printed in the United States of America

1 2 3 4 5 6 7 8 9 02 01 00 99 98

Front cover: Silver **mane** and tail streaming, golden and graceful, Palominos are the showstoppers of the horse world.

TABLE OF CONTENTS

Words that appear in the glossary are printed in **boldface** type the first time they occur in the text.

THE FIRST GOLD IN CALIFORNIA?

Some people say the first Palomino was **bred** by Don Estaban, a cattleman of Old California. In 1800, Don Estaban told all his workers, "I will pay much silver to the one who brings me the most beautiful horse in the country." He did not know he would receive gold for his offer of silver!

One young boy carefully looked over all the horses that were rounded up during the grain harvest. He picked a stallion (male horse) he knew would win. Then he washed and polished his find. When the boy showed the horse to Don Estaban, the horse's mane and tail shone silver, and its coat gleamed gold. The stallion had many **foals** (baby horses), which also had its fine gold color.

Outshining the rest of the herd, the Palomino's beauty cannot fail to catch our attention.

A PALOMINO ISN'T . . .

Almost any **registered horse breed** can also be a Palomino, but not all gold-colored horses are Palominos.

A registered horse breed is a group of horses that all have the same physical features because people select and **breed** them for those features. To be registered as a breed, a horse's **conformation** must agree with the rules laid down by that breed's association.

Gold-colored horses with black or striped manes, blue eyes, spotted skin, dappled or streaked hair and tails, and white coats are *not* Palominos.

Many features can disqualify a horse that otherwise looks like a Palomino. This horse may be the right color, but the stripe on its back is a Palomino no-no!

A PALOMINO IS . . .

American Saddlebreds, Thoroughbreds, American Standardbreds, Morgans, Quarter Horses, Arabians, and Tennessee Walking Horses — all are registered American horse breeds that can also be Palominos.

To be a Palomino, a horse must have a coat close to the color of a "newly-minted American gold dollar." It must have dark or golden skin under its gold hair. A Palomino may also have white leg markings up to its knees.

A Palomino's mane and tail must be white with close to fifteen black strands for every eighty-five white strands. The black strands are almost impossible to see unless you look closely.

Horses from many breeds can be Palominos. This horse looks like a Saddlebred being used for Western Pleasure Riding.

LET'S FACE IT!

To be a Palomino, a horse may only have certain white markings on its face. It may have a star, a snip, a stripe, or a blaze. A star is a patch on the forehead. A snip is a patch on the nose between the nostrils. A stripe looks as though a line is painted from between the ears to the nostrils. A blaze is a wider stripe that touches the rims of the nostrils.

Palominos may not have what is known as a bald face. This does not mean that some horses have faces with no hair at all! If a horse has a bald face, it may have some colored hair on its cheeks and its ears, but the rest of the hair on its face is white.

This Palomino has a star on its forehead and a snip between its nostrils. Notice the dark skin around its **muzzle** and eyes.

PROSPECTING FOR GOLD

When a horse is bred, a person selects a mare (a female horse) and a stallion to **mate** and have foals together. The mare and stallion are chosen because of special features they or their parents have.

After their birth, the foals are examined to see if they have all the right features. If a foal is missing even one feature, it cannot be registered as a Palomino. Even if both parents are Palominos, there is no guarantee of Palomino foals.

In fact, a Palomino stallion and a Palomino mare have true Palomino foals only half of the time. Another quarter of their foals will be creamy white with blue eyes. The rest will be light red with dark skin, or **red dun**.

This jumper has all the right stuff to be registered as a Palomino. Now for the other obstacles in its path!

NOT ALL THAT GLITTERS . . .

Can Palominos be bred from horses of different colors? Yes! Palominos are really pale red horses. Most Palomino foals are bred from rust-colored horses like chestnuts or sorrels.

Breeders figured this out. They bred **cremellos** (pale yellow horses) with chestnuts and got Palomino-colored foals every time. But cremellos are a kind of albino (a colorless horse), which are not allowed.

Can a Palomino foal have a black parent? It can! Some black horses have the makings of Palominos in their blood. With all these choices, breeders have to work hard to breed foals the color of "newly-minted gold"!

The horse in front is a chestnut Tennessee Walker with a light mane and tail. Although its coat is a dark color, a careful breeder might "strike" gold.

GOLD STARS OF THE SILVER SCREEN

Many Palominos were movie stars. A Palomino named Tarzan, who was also half Arabian and half American Saddlebred, costarred with actor Ken Maynard in movies of the 1930s.

Tarzan did so many tricks that Ken often changed the movie scripts to get Tarzan's tricks into the story. The Palomino danced, bowed, rolled over and played dead, nodded his head to answer questions, and rang fire alarms.

In their movies together, Tarzan saved Ken from dangers such as fire, quicksand, and outlaws. Tarzan was the first famous Palomino movie star. He often went on road shows to meet his fans.

William Rice Burroughs, author of books about Tarzan, the Apeman, was a friend of Ken Maynard *(pictured)*. Burroughs admired Ken's heroic horse and named him Tarzan.

HORSING AROUND ON TV

Palominos have been part of many television series. But one Palomino, Mr. Ed, had his own show. Mr. Ed played a talking horse. He was a horse, of course, but he couldn't really talk. Mr. Ed moved his lips just like he was talking, and a voice actor behind the scenes spoke his lines for him.

Still, Mr. Ed was very smart. He could nod and shake his head, lie down, whinny and neigh, curl his lips, and pick things up with his teeth and then carry them around.

Besides, he could always get Wilbur (his "master" on the show) out of trouble.

Scientists who study horses say that horses smell each other's breath in order to recognize each other. What do you imagine Mr. Ed thought of Wilbur's breath?

DRESSED FOR SUCCESS

Palominos do many kinds of work. It all depends on what strengths and skills their parents gave them. Palominos work on cattle ranches as bulldoggers (horses that herd cattle). They are show horses in **dressage**, jumping, and Western and English Pleasure Riding. Some are polo ponies, and others are parade horses. They are all "dressed for success" in their beautiful gold and silver suits.

You can find a Palomino for just about any kind of job a horse can do, because its parents might be any kind of registered breed.

Basically, each Palomino is a different horse of the same color.

Whether riders clear a water jump or not, they'll make a splash on a horse of silver and gold.

DIAGRAM AND SCALE OF A HORSE

Here's how to measure a horse with a show of hands.
This Palomino has all the right stuff. See if you can
list the features that make an ideal Palomino.

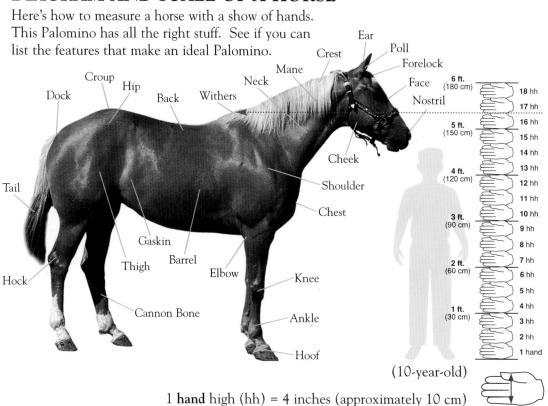

Ear
Poll
Forelock
Crest
Face
Mane
Neck
Nostril
Croup
Hip
Dock
Back
Withers
Cheek
Shoulder
Chest
Tail
Gaskin
Thigh
Barrel
Elbow
Knee
Hock
Cannon Bone
Ankle
Hoof

6 ft. (180 cm) — 18 hh, 17 hh
5 ft. (150 cm) — 16 hh, 15 hh, 14 hh
4 ft. (120 cm) — 13 hh, 12 hh, 11 hh
3 ft. (90 cm) — 10 hh, 9 hh, 8 hh
2 ft. (60 cm) — 7 hh, 6 hh, 5 hh
1 ft. (30 cm) — 4 hh, 3 hh, 2 hh, 1 hand

(10-year-old)

1 **hand** high (hh) = 4 inches (approximately 10 cm)

WHERE TO WRITE OR CALL FOR MORE INFORMATION

Palomino Horse Breeders of America
15253 East Skeely Drive
Tulsa, OK 74116-1234
Phone: (918) 438-1234

22

MORE TO READ AND VIEW

Books (Nonfiction): *The Complete Guides to Horses and Ponies* (series). Jackie Budd
(Gareth Stevens)
Great American Horses (series). Victor Gentle and Janet Perry
(Gareth Stevens)
Horses. Animal Families (series). Hans Dossenbach (Gareth Stevens)
Magnificent Horses of the World (series). Tomáš Míček and
Dr. Hans-Jörg Schrenk (Gareth Stevens)
Wild Horse Magic for Kids. Animal Magic (series). Mark Henckel
(Gareth Stevens)
Wild Horses of the Red Desert. Glen Rounds (Holiday House)

Books (Fiction): *Golden Arrow*. B. Holland Heck (Scribner Press)
Herds of Thunder, Manes of Gold. Edited by B. Coville (Doubleday)
Saddle Club (series). Bonnie Bryant (Gareth Stevens)
Wild Palomino: Stallion of the Prairies. Stephen Holt
(Grosset & Dunlap)

Videos (Fiction): *The Black Stallion*. (MGM Home Video)
Justin Morgan Had a Horse. (Walt Disney)

WEB SITES

For Palomino information:
palominohba.com/youthhome.htm

For interactive games:
www.haynet.net/kidstuff.html

For general horse information:
www.haynet.net
www.bcm.nt
okstate.edu/breeds/horses

Due to the dynamic nature of the Internet, some web sites stay current longer than others.
To find additional web sites, use a reliable search engine with one or more of the following
keywords to help you locate information about horses: *Arabians, equitation, Quarter Horses,
racing, Tennessee Walking Horses,* and *Thoroughbreds.*

GLOSSARY

You can find these words on the pages listed. Reading a word in a sentence helps you understand it even better.

breed (v), **bred** — to choose a stallion and a mare with certain features to produce foals with similar features 4, 6, 12, 14

conformation (KON-for-MAY-shun) — how a horse's body is built 6

cremello (cree-MEL-o) — a horse with yellowish white hair and maybe blue or dark eyes 14

dressage (druh-SAHJ) — training a horse to perform gaits in an orderly way 20

foals (FOHLZ) — baby horses 4, 12, 14

hand — a unit to measure horses that is equal to the width of a human hand, about 4 inches (10.2 cm) 22

mane — the long hair that grows from the head and neck of a horse 2, 4, 6, 8, 14

mate — to join (animals) together to produce young 12

muzzle — the jaws and nose of an animal 10

red dun — a horse with dark skin and a reddish coat 12

registered horse breed — a breed that follows certain rules set by that particular breed's association 6, 8, 12, 14, 20

INDEX